What Did Jesus Say About Prayer?

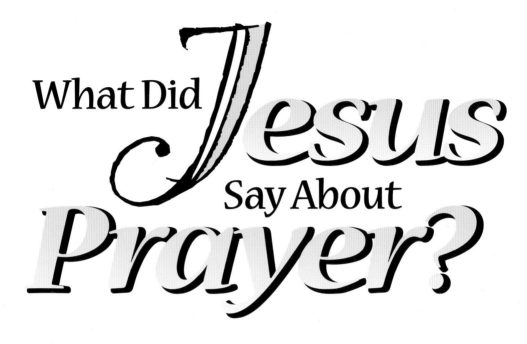

By Helen Haidle

Illustrated by Cheri Bladholm

Zonderkidz™

DEDICATION

To Keith and Judy Reetz
Thank you for all your prayers
for the children and youth of this generation.
Your faithfulness to pray is a blessing to many.

Helen Haidle

To Ann and Frank Colabufo
and their children,
Nathan, Meghan, Samuel,
who were adopted from Korea,
and to baby Daniel.

These children were gifts from God
given in answer to prayer.

Your faith inspires me.

Cheri Bladholm

What Did Jesus Say About Prayer?
ISBN: 0-310-70022-1
Copyright © 2002 by Helen Haidle
Illustrations copyright © 2002 by Cheri Bladholm

Zonderkidz™

The children's group of Zondervan

Requests for information should be addressed to:
Grand Rapids, Michigan 49530
www.zonderkidz.com

All Scripture quotations, unless otherwise indicated, are taken from Holy Bible, New International Reader's Version ®
Copyright © 1994, 1996 by International Bible Society. Used by permission of Zondervan.

Interior design by Lisa Workman
Art direction by Jody Langley
Edited by Gwen Ellis

Printed in Hong Kong
02 03 04 05/HK/5 4 3 2 1

Who is Jesus?

Jesus is the Son of God. He prayed to his heavenly Father. Jesus also wants us to pray.

"After Jesus had sent the crowd away, he went up on a mountainside by himself to pray."

Matthew 14:23

Jesus said,

"Father, I thank you

for hearing me.

I know that you

always hear me."

John 11:41-42

God loves you. God wants you to talk to him. Take time every day to tell him your feelings. Thank him. Share your joys and your problems. You can be sure that God hears you.

Jesus said,

"You know how to

give good gifts to

your children. How

much more will

your Father who is

in heaven give good

gifts to those

who ask him!"

Matthew 7:11

A loving daddy knows what to give his children. God is the best Father who gives the best gifts. God wants you to come to him in prayer.

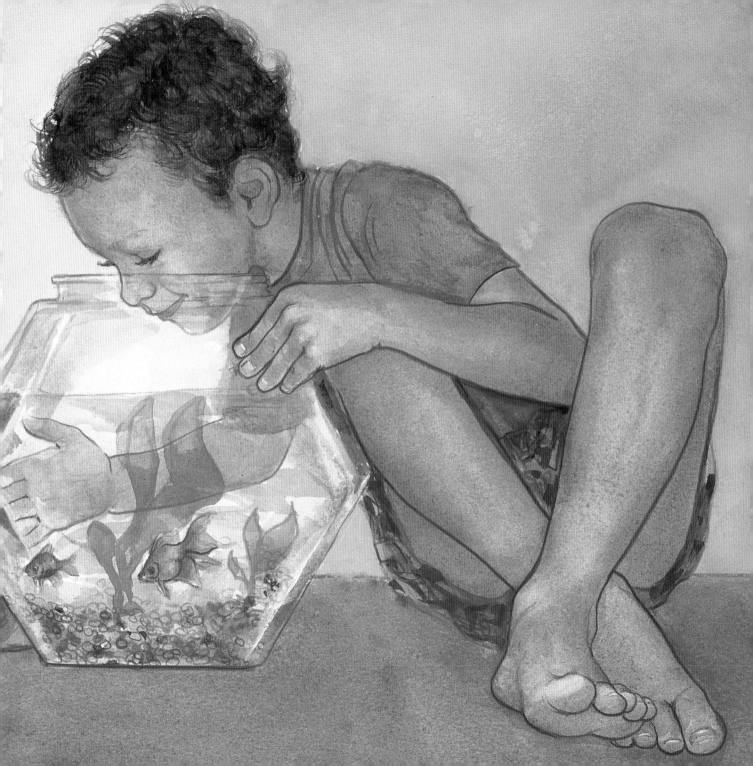

Jesus said,

"Ask, and it shall

be given to you....

Everyone who asks

will receive."

Matthew 7:7-8

Don't get discouraged when your work seems too hard. Don't give up when it seems like God doesn't answer. Jesus wants you to keep on praying.

Jesus said,

"So I tell you, when

you pray for

something, believe

that you have

already received

it. Then it will

be yours."

Mark 11:24

Jesus wants you to trust and believe in him. Whenever you need help—pray! Depend on his help before you get an answer. Never doubt that Jesus can do what you ask.

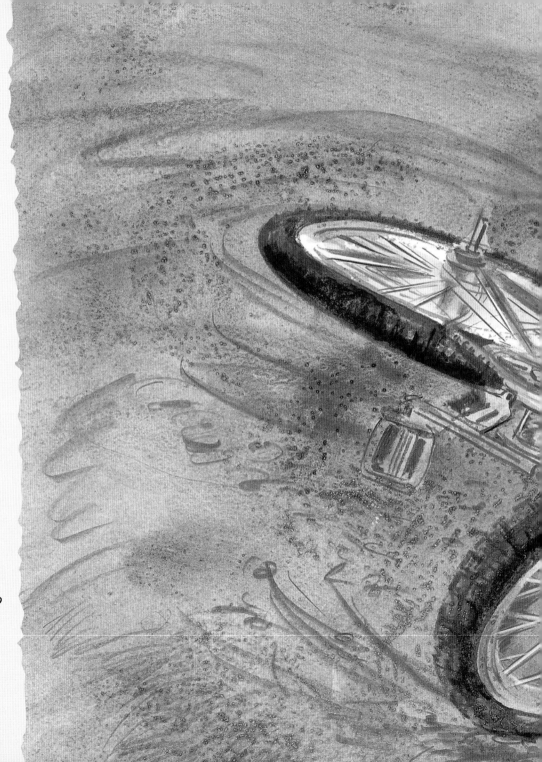

Jesus said,

"When you pray, do
not keep talking on
and on the way
ungodly people do.
They think they will
be heard because
they talk alot...Your
Father knows what
you need even
before you ask him."

Matthew 6:7-8

God knows all your problems before you pray. So don't worry about what to say to him. It doesn't matter if your prayer is short or long. Just tell God what you need.

Be willing to pray with other people. When you pray with your family and friends, you can be sure that Jesus is there, too.

Jesus said,

"Suppose two of you

on earth agree

about anything you

ask for. My Father

in heaven will do it

for you. Where two

or three people

meet together in

my name, I am

there with them."

Matthew 18:19-20

Jesus said,

"When you pray, go

into your room.

Close the door and

pray to your

Father, who can't

be seen. He will

reward you. Your

Father sees what is

done secretly."

Matthew 6:6

*T*ake time to be all by yourself with God. Find a place where you can pray secretly. Pray out loud or pray silently. God sees you and hears you.

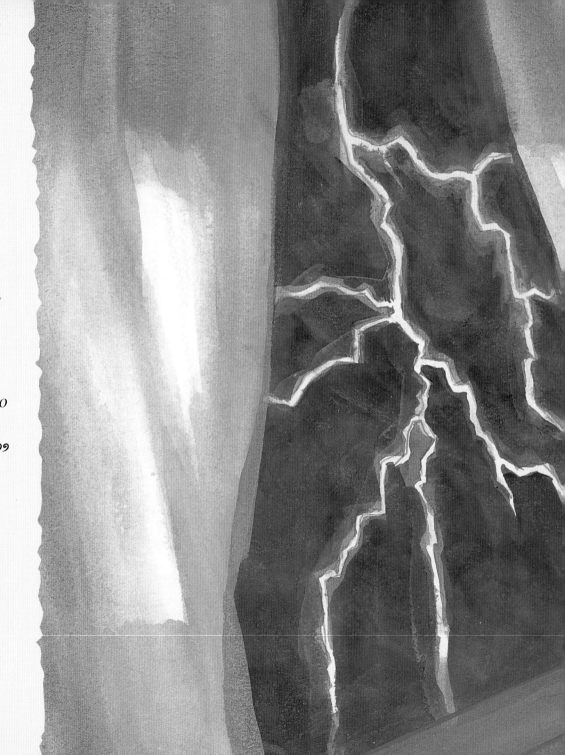

Jesus said,

" I tell you, do not

worry. Put God's

kingdom first. Do

what he wants you

to do. Then all of

those things will also

be given to you. "

Matthew 6:25,33

Whenever you feel worried—pray! Give God first place in your life. Stay close to him in prayer. He will take care of you.

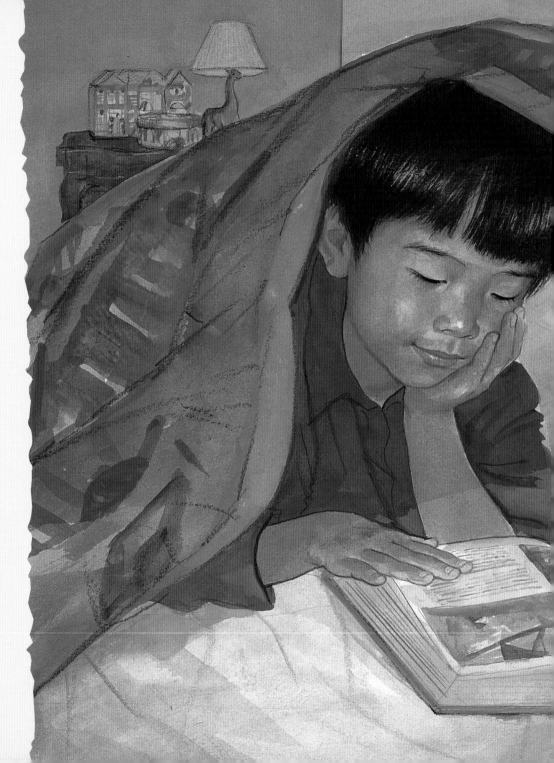

Jesus said,
"You can't do
anything without
me. If you remain
joined to me and my
words remain in
you, ask for
anything you wish
and it will be given
to you."

John 15:5,7

Jesus wants to be part of everything you do. So read your Bible and get to know him. Talk to Jesus about anything. He will answer your prayers.

Jesus said,

"I will do anything

you ask in my

name....You may

ask me for

anything in my

name.

I will do it."

John 14:13-14

Jesus gave his life for you. He loves you! That is why you can go to him in prayer. Jesus invites you to pray about everything. And he promises to answer you.

Jesus said,

"Here is what I tell

you. Love your

enemies. Pray for

those who hurt

you. Then you will

be sons of your

Father who is

in heaven."

Matthew 5:44-45

Don't just pray for your family and friends. Pray for people who are mean to you. Jesus prayed for those who crucified him.

Jesus said,

"When you stand praying, forgive anyone you have anything against. Then your Father in heaven will forgive your sins."

Mark 11:25

When you pray, don't hold a grudge against others. Be willing to forgive those who have hurt you. Remember that you need God's forgiveness, too.

Jesus prayed, "Father, if you are willing, take this cup of suffering away from me. But do what you want, not what I want."

Luke 22:42

God may answer your prayers differently than you expect. You can trust that God always knows what is best. God did not take away Jesus' pain and suffering, but Jesus accepted God's answer of "No."

Jesus said,

"The harvest is huge.

But there are only a

few workers. So

ask the Lord of the

harvest to send

workers out into his

harvest field."

Matthew 9:37–38

Jesus compared the world to a field of ripe grain. Many people are waiting to hear about Jesus. You can ask God to send workers all over the world to teach people about Jesus.

The disciples of Jesus watched him pray. They asked Jesus to teach them to pray. And he told them to pray in this way:

"Our Father in heaven, may your name be honored. May your kingdom come. May what you want to happen be done on earth as it is done in heaven. Give us today our daily bread. Forgive us our sins, just as we also have forgiven those who sin against us. Keep us from falling into sin when we are tempted. Save us from the evil one."

Matthew 6:9-13